D1710429

THE GOMER ANOINTING

A Calling to Deliver a Nation

STACIA V. HUNTER

WESTBOW
PRESS®
A DIVISION OF THOMAS NELSON
& ZONDERVAN

Scripture taken from the King James Version of the Bible.
Scripture taken from the New King James Version®. Copyright © 1982
by Thomas Nelson. Used by permission. All rights reserved.
THE HOLY BIBLE, NEW INTERNATIONAL VERSION®,
NIV® Copyright © 1973, 1978, 1984, 2011 by Biblica, Inc.®
Used by permission. All rights reserved worldwide.

WestBow Press books may be ordered through booksellers or by contacting:

WestBow Press
A Division of Thomas Nelson & Zondervan
1663 Liberty Drive
Bloomington, IN 47403
www.westbowpress.com
1 (866) 928-1240

Because of the dynamic nature of the Internet, any web addresses or
links contained in this book may have changed since publication and
may no longer be valid. The views expressed in this work are solely those
of the author and do not necessarily reflect the views of the publisher,
and the publisher hereby disclaims any responsibility for them.

Any people depicted in stock imagery provided by Getty Images are
models, and such images are being used for illustrative purposes only.
Certain stock imagery © Getty Images.

ISBN: 978-1-9736-4925-0 (sc)
ISBN: 978-1-9736-4926-7 (e)

Library of Congress Control Number: 2018914891

Print information available on the last page.

WestBow Press rev. date: 1/11/2019

Contents

Dedication

All of the glory, the honor, and my praise are rendered to the true and living God. He is my source and my life; therefore, I dedicate this inspired work to His glory and for the good of all who read it. I also dedicate this book to the wonderful memories and the fortified legacy of my grandparents, the late Hoover Sr. and Mildred Hunter. I also dedicate this book to my family, in particular, my mother, Delores H. McKinnis. Thank you, Mom, for always sending me to the dictionary. It was the first building block in my writing skills. I am a fruit of your good works. This book is also dedicated to my siblings, nieces, and nephews. I love you all!

Introduction

IS GOMER FIT TO LEAD WORSHIP?

And the Spirit and the bride say, Come.
And let him that heareth say, Come. And
whosoever will, let him take the water of
life freely.

—Revelation 22:17 (KJV)

I have spent a lot time while in meditation with God asking questions. I believe that in order for a believer to grow closer to God, he or she must seek Him to understand Him and His ways more fully. As we gain greater understanding, we, in turn, understand our own purpose on earth. This also causes us to more deeply appreciate the purposes of our brothers and sisters in Christ Jesus.

We each have a unique love story, which involves God. No story is the same. Some of us have simply stumbled upon His love and have been greatly overwhelmed. Others have heard about God and His redeeming power from their parents or grandparents, who dragged them to church. Then there are those in the body of Christ who have not been able to grasp the concept, let alone the reality, of God's love for them because no one in their family had any real relationship with God.

Thankfully, by grace through faith, we are saved and not by ourselves. According to Ephesians 2:8–9 (NKJV), "We are His workmanship, created in Christ Jesus for good works, which God prepared beforehand that we should walk in them." This great love cannot be earned but is a gift from God, and therefore, we have initiated nothing. Simply put, we are responding to God's awesome and redeeming love.

In the history of love stories, one of the most incredible and heartbreaking ones is about the enduring love Hosea had for Gomer, which is found in the Old Testament. Typically, when we speak of this love story, we hear the exposé of Hosea the prophet whom God instructed to marry a "wife of harlotry," for the land had committed harlotry. According to Hosea 1:2 (KJV),

"Hosea who was the son of Beeri, went and took Gomer the daughter of Diblaim as a wife." The book of Hosea is a narrative that is bursting with prophetic and poetic intent, which mirrors the divine romance between God and His covenant people. (1.)

Hosea's heart was filled with love and fervent obedience to God, which resulted in him and Gomer having three children. Each birth spoke prophetically, with each child carrying a symbolic name from the Lord.

Their son Jezreel, who was the firstborn, was given a name reflecting the past atrocities that had occurred at Jezreel. He was also given this name as a reminder to Israel that God's judgement was sure to come quickly as He had promised it would.

Their second oldest was a daughter, Lo-Ruhamah, whose name meant *not loved*. Wow. This was God declaring to Israel that He had taken away His love.

Hosea and Gomer's last child was Lo-Ammi, whose name means *not my people*. This name served to represent God's withdrawal of His relationship with Israel, which was covenantal.

I was led into a deep and revelatory study of God's Word after receiving a rhema word from the Lord upon asking Him questions. Can you visualize how shameful and humiliating this was for Hosea? His assignment was to denounce sin, to warn others of God's pronounced judgement, and to proclaim to the faithful that God would reign over them with unlimited compassion and love. (1.)

This is such an awesome story of unconditional love with a deep underlying prophetic message. I went deep into the book of Hosea and its rich interpretation of God's unconditional and redemptive love, which would war and win against Israel's revolting idolatry. (1.)

I was at a place of frustration as I queried the Lord regarding my witnessing the extreme competitiveness and judgmental postures among a group of leaders in the body of Christ. This incident occurred after a very powerful and supernatural move of God. The experience was so humbling and overwhelming, I found myself pronouncing a profound testimonial to the worship leaders regarding the importance of pure obedience. Before I knew it, I spoke these words: "This move of God manifested through the obedience of our leader."

After my statement, the atmosphere became tense, and then a disconnection occurred in the midst of this group of worshippers. I didn't understand why. Why were there such baffling looks? Why was there such painstaking silence? Right there in that moment, the Spirit of the Lord answered me and said, "They have issues with Gomer leading them."

My initial thought was, *Gomer? Why Gomer? Gomer was a prostitute. Gomer was considered a woman of low worth, full of undignified characteristics.* Then I understood that the Spirit of the Lord was referring to her past life. Certainly, after pondering through this sister's past, I will admit, yes, she was something in her day but so were some of you.

It was amazing and saddening to me that we were at a paramount in our ministry as a group, after many trials, tribulations, and even the death of one of our cohorts, and yet we still could not acknowledge the need for the true refinement of each leader in Christ Jesus. How could the dear saints who labored in ministry with this anointed vessel of God still say in their hearts, *She cannot lead me anywhere!* while prospering in the benefits of her anointing and her obedience.

The thoughts we sometimes have toward one another are somewhat appalling. We all have been found guilty of unfairly painting people's lives with the sinful brush of their pasts. Even I, at times, have been shamefaced because of my participation in this unfruitful part of church culture. So this was an awesome revelation that broke strongholds off me and freed me from my past.

We all have a past, go through a process, and are forgiven. God has a purpose and a plan for us, even for someone who has had a sordid past like Gomer. The men, women, money, drugs, and games that have been played still do not outweigh the calling on a person's life.

The Holy Spirit took me through a series of questions when I began writing this book. I was at a women's conference where a single minister from the community led the people in worship.

The Spirit said to me, "What if I told you to marry him?"

I was dumbfounded and horrified all at the same time! I stopped worshipping with my hands and went deeper into my thoughts and conversation with the Spirit of the Lord. "Oh, Lord!"

The Spirit spoke again and said, "Is he not Gomer?"

I dropped my head while others were being led into the presence of God by this anointed worship leader. I knew some things about his past and God revealed other things in that moment that were not honorable for a minister. Then I repented and said to the Spirit of God, "If it be Your will, Lord, I will obey."

This brings me to my second revelation, which came through my conversations with the Holy Spirit. There is an underlying distain in the body of Christ for the reformed Gomer. The church holds the former lives of reformed Gomers against them, thereby holding the gifts, which are needed for the body's edification, hostage. Therefore, the saints are damming up the flow of the anointing simply because they are offended by what God has delivered a person from. The saints are then guilty of watering down God's supernatural power, which is working, setting free, and delivering people.

It is very wrong for the members of Christ's body to exalt their thinking and ways above God's ways. Isaiah 55:8–9 (NIV), "'My thoughts are nothing like your thoughts,' says the Lord. 'And my ways are far beyond anything you could imagine.'"

This reminds me of the arrogance and rebellion found in the book of Jonah. He was a prophet of God who was bound to the past hurts of his people and did not want to see God's grace, compassion, and salvation poured out on the people of Nineveh. Therefore, he exalted one people over another and held God's blessings for ransom.

Even in silence, our pride can be very harmful to the body of believers and the generation at hand, which is already weary of the rejection it finds in the church. We, as the church, must receive freedom from religious strongholds that hinder us.

Can Gomer lead worship? Is Gomer called to preach? How can this be? I remember praying for Gomer and her dirty little secrets just five years ago. Has she really been delivered from the former lifestyle, which even she, at one point in time, doubted she would ever be delivered from?

She has finally surrendered completely to God's will for her life. So why aren't we encouraging Gomer in her deliverance and anointing? We are witnesses to Gomer's flourishing purpose. Shouldn't we be happy? Have we been misled by our own deceit into believing that the reformed Gomer can never be used by God to help bring forth His kingdom? Gomer, in a delivered state, is equipped to carry the anointing and the glory of God. She has value and virtue. Let's explore it.

Chapter 1

Gomer's Debaucheries Versus Hosea's Obedience

Against you, you only, have I sinned and done what is evil in your sight; so you are right in your verdict and justified when you judge.

—Psalm 51:4 (NIV)

Please do not be offended by the questions you are about to read. This book was not written to offend. It was written to open the readers' minds so that they could see and understand their authentic selves and how our loving and faithful God assesses them through His love and the blood of Jesus. So with that said, are you a reformed Gomer? Are you a secret Gomer who is still living in spiritual harlotry? Perhaps you are a skeptic of Gomer and her deliverance altogether.

When we sin, we sin against God alone. Unfortunately, we tend to cast a brighter light on the sins of others and see these sins as being greater than our own. Gomer is no different. She has been talked about for more than two thousand years. However, in the examination of Gomer's sins, we can see some parallels to our own sins and shortcomings, rather than pointing fingers at the vagarious life of a prostitute.

When you think about it, Gomer wasn't just any prostitute. She was a prostitute whom God had ordained to be loved by the man of God, Hosea. What an assignment. God had ordained their relationship so that the glory of the Lord would be revealed. This was a phenomenal work of the Lord. It was a relationship miracle orchestrated by God and carried out by His obedient prophet. When we take a closer look, we understand that the biblical Gomer's value was never diminished in the eyes of her devoted husband or a faithful God she did not truly know.

Maybe there has been a time in your life when you were considered a spiritual Gomer. When I was a young adult, I desired a deeper relationship with God. I only had judgmental church people telling me what I could not do and who I was not fit to marry. I was crushed. I thought, *So why come to church if I will never be fit enough to become part of the body?*

No one told me in those years that I was fearfully and wonderfully made. They didn't say that God had cleansed me from all my sins and that He loved me. People were too busy talking about my denominational background, whether or not I was dating, and my family history. Of course, they also discussed my sins and shortcomings and made up rumors about me. As a result, no one stopped to tell me that God's amazing grace and love were stronger than my sins and their residue were.

WHO ARE YOU CALLING GOMER?

Of course, it is not politically correct to refer to someone as Gomer. That statement would bring great shame on a person if it was directed in a derogatory way.

Gomer's debaucheries were quite offensive, and she was extremely intoxicated with them. Gomer, the wife of Hosea the prophet and the harlot that everyone knew, was enslaved in her own heart by her sins. The sins of Gomer, the adulterous bride, were simply irrefutable. She openly adorned herself with her perverseness and sensual desires. She was a prostitute in a land that worshipped the idols of the Phoenicians—largely those of the Tyrians and including Baal. Through this profane worship, great solemnities and ritual harlotries became the standard amid the Hebrews, particularly in Samaria.

Deuteronomy 23:17–18 (NKJV) says, "There shall be no ritual harlot of the daughters of Israel, or a perverted one of the sons of Israel. You shall not bring the wage of a harlot or the price of a dog to the house of the Lord your God for any vowed offering for both of these are an abomination to the Lord your God." Clearly, you can hear the indignation in this scripture. It was blatant disobedience to be a temple harlot. Therefore, Gomer's profane worship and her sexual yearning kept her as a spiritual vagabond who consistently abandoned her committed husband—along with her children.

Have you played the harlot as Gomer did? It seems unimaginable to find yourself in the shoes of a harlot. It's an unclean and shameful lifestyle. How can God love a person who has been persistently wicked and is seemingly unredeemable? Is there true deliverance for the harlot? Can the unfaithful be reconciled back to a holy God?

Hear the prophetic word of the Lord in Hosea 2:15 (NKJV): "Therefore, behold, I will allure her, will bring her into the wilderness, and speak comfort to her, I will give her vineyards from there, and the Valley of Achor as a door of hope." According to Jeremiah 3:14, God is married to the backslider, so yes, He can return to us and turn us back to Himself. Every day, He is wooing the lost back into His arms of safety from the desolate life of exile.

In the same way that it was heartbreaking for Hosea to see Gomer enslaved by her transgressions, it was also heartbreaking for God to see Israel's rejection of His everlasting love. Hosea 4:12 (NKJV) says, "My people ask counsel from their wooden idols, and their staff informs them. For the spirit of harlotry has caused them to stray. And they have played the harlot against their God."

Even in the haze of Israel's idolatry, the sovereignty of God and His love was truly amazing. He, just like Hosea, chased those who were overwhelmed and seduced by sin, shame, and the lust of their flesh, which was no match for God's unconditional love. Yes, God absolutely hates sin, and thankfully, He seeks His people with redeemable love.

Hosea 3:1–3 (NKJV) says,

> Then the Lord said to me, "Go again, love a woman who is loved by a lover and is committing adultery, just like the love of the Lord for the children of Israel, who look to other gods and love the raisin cakes of pagans." So I bought her for myself for fifteen shekels of silver, and one and one-half homers of barley. And I said to her, "You shall stay with me many days; you shall not play the harlot, nor shall you have a man—so, too, will I be toward you."

Hosea's Gomer had uncontrolled passion that led her back and forth through a trench of debauchery under the influence of her possessor, Baal. Even her motherhood could not sober her thinking or motivate her to surrender to the God of Israel.

WHY WON'T GOMER COME HOME?

In my studies, I was puzzled as to why Gomer would not return to her home when she had the chance. Why wouldn't she want to stay in a warm and safe environment with someone as faithful as Hosea? He had proven, over and over again, he would do anything for her. Being a mother who had given birth to three children, who may or may not have been Hosea's, why didn't she stay to raise her children? Why didn't she stay to love her children?

The Spirit of God revealed to my heart that while Gomer was in her sin, she did not have the capacity to love anyone because she didn't love herself. Coming home to Hosea and her children was uncomfortable and unbearable because she knew the depth of her unworthiness: to be loved, cared for, respected, and given dignity by her husband. Hosea provided Gomer with a life that she did not deserve.

Gomer was broken and in a constant search to medicate her pain and to fill a void that was created by fear, complacency, and low self-worth and self-esteem. She was in a pit of shame and disillusionment that became deeper after each birth. With every sexual performance, she brought glory to an idol that could not save her soul or quench the fire of her insatiable heart.

Israel, in its passion for Baal, also lost the blessings of the Lord as it searched for the false fruitfulness and prosperity of a dumb idol. Hosea 2:1–5 (NKJV) says,

> Bring charges against you mother, bring charges; for she is not My wife, not am I her Husband! Let her put away her harlotries from her sight, And her adulteries from between her breast; Lest I strip her naked and expose her, as in the day she was born, and make her like a wilderness, and set her like a dry land, and slay her with thirst. I will not have mercy on her children, for they are the children of harlotry. For their mother has played the harlot; she who conceived them has behaved shamefully. For she said, I will go after my lovers, Who give me bread and my water, My wool and my linen, my oil and my drink.

Why was Gomer so fervent for the life of a harlot and the darkness of Baal and Astarte? Historically, in theological texts of the book of Hosea, Baal was the most important deity in the Canaanite pantheon. This heretical movement was so successful because it held the belief that idols of Baal would bring fertility to the land every spring. The ceremonial sacrifices and worship were typically sexual in nature.

According to Hosea 4:12–14, the young men and women were taught that they would gain favor through baalism and that their ritualistic prostitution would give them the ability to produce and bear children. Some of the gods of baalism included El (father of the gods), Asherah (mother goddess), Baal (god of weather), Baal's partner, Astarte (goddess of fertility), and Mot (god of death).

While considering the historical and theological standpoint of the story of Hosea and Gomer, I gained the understanding that Gomer's passion came from a generational seed of heresy that had been ingrained in Israel's hearts and minds. The Israelites had departed from the Lord their God, to seek the prosperity of the great weather god of the western Semites.

The average Baal worshipper depended on rain. They viewed rain as the abundance of Baal and were known to eat sacrifices for the dead in honor of Baal. Therefore, the ways of Baal were all Gomer had known. How could she even conceive Hosea's true and living God?

GOMER'S SIN NATURE

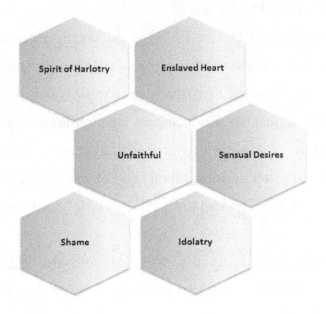

Spirit of Harlotry

Enslaved Heart

Unfaithful

Sensual Desires

Shame

Idolatry

Even though the biblical Gomer's sin nature was great, I believe that the phenomenal grace that was present in Gomer's life and in this love story is a great illustration of God's *special grace*, which would one day be poured out over rebellious Israel through the blood of a redeeming Savior. God redeems, sanctifies, and glorifies His people with this reforming theology. Unlike common grace, which is universally given, special grace is bestowed only on those God elects to received eternal life through faith in Jesus. This grace, which relates to our eternal salvation, is present today and working in our lives.

Romans 6:23 (NIV) says, "For the wages of sin is death, but the gift of God is eternal life in Christ Jesus our Lord." Therefore, God offered Gomer grace and the gift of eternal life rather than a deserving death. Why would God offer grace to someone who had taken advantage of His love repeatedly?

Does this remind you of yourself? We live under a better covenant of grace than Gomer did, who lived before the coming of the Messiah. So when we think about it, we are really without excuse when it comes to being a repeat offender. As a matter of fact, we fear that our own love will be rejected by those whom we have entrusted it to. Even those who are faithful fall back into patterns of unfaithfulness to God, His will, and His ways. Gomer's sin nature is no different from our own.

Overall, when we ponder the complexity of Gomer's entrapment in iniquity, we have to wonder what she had to lose. Why couldn't she see the magnificent gains in her path by surrendering to the love of her husband and his God. It's hard to imagine not having the capacity to love or to receive love on that level.

1 John 4:7–10 (ESV) says,

> Beloved, let us love one another, for love is from God, and whoever loves has been born of God and knows God. Anyone who does not love does not know God, because God is love. In this the love of God, was made manifest among us, that God send His only Son into the world, so that we might live through Him. In this is love, not that we have loved God but that He loved us and sent His Son to be the propitiation for our sins.

Chapter 2

AGONIZING REJECTION: HOSEA'S PRAYER LIFE

"And it shall be, in that day," Says that Lord, "That you will call Me 'My Husband,' And no longer call Me 'My Master,' For I will take from her mouth the names of the Baals, And they shall be remembered by their name no more."

—Hosea 2:16–17 (NKJV)

It is a husband's job to protect, to lead, and to make his wife and family secure. As a husband, Hosea had all of these qualities. As a man of God, he had even more. There is no doubt that when Gomer abandoned her family, he prayed for her. He prayed for her protection and that her eyes would be opened so that she could see that he was her husband and that his love was true. He wanted her to see that she could never fill the void in her heart by worshipping Baal.

While praying, Hosea prophesied the deliverance of Gomer. He had to travail for Gomer time and time again. He had a mandate from the Lord not to give up on her.

Hosea prayed that his wife would only have eyes for him and would love her family enough to come home and stay with them. He prayed that God would forgive her, turn her away from her false gods, grant her mercy and grace in spite of her immeasurable sins, and restore her as only He could restore His chosen people. He cried out to God for his children, who had been abandoned by their mother and couldn't even love herself. He prayed that he would remain faithful and loving to his unfaithful and unloving wife. He prayed for his own heartbreak and grief because he was a rejected man.

I can only imagine how he would have felt. He might have felt emasculated, shameful, and abandoned. He might even have been viewed as insane for continuing to go and rescue Gomer, who didn't want to be saved. He put everything he had into freeing her and buying her back. It would have been a most humiliating circumstance, which would have kept him humble in prayer and obedience when God said, "Go again. Love a woman who is loved by a lover and is committing adultery just like Israel." This was the ultimate act of mercy. His love for Gomer was to mirror the love that God had for the children of Israel, who also didn't realize that they were lost.

So what can we learn and apply to the body of Christ from Hosea's actions? First, love the person and not the sin. You've heard that before. In the midst of a person's sinful behavior, you have to present true and authentic love that will penetrate his or her heart. Only the love of God can do that. Secondly, humble yourself. Do not operate out of pride by putting a time limit on that person. Deliverance takes time, and you may have to walk with a person for a long season before he or she truly receives even a portion of what God has for that person. Thirdly, obey God. The Spirit of the Lord will do the deep work. You are to walk in obedience and love.

PRAYING FOR GOMER

Dear God,

Help me to love him/her even though he/she doesn't love me. Lord, I need Your help. He/She doesn't value me. He/She doesn't value what I give or what I say. Please root out the unforgiveness in me. Help him/her to see my value and not to be intimidated by me and the love I have for him/her. Let him/her not only value what I can do but also who I am in You. Open his/her spiritual eyes and ears. Root out stubbornness from both of us and release Your kindness and love among us. Lord, in the strong name of Jesus, bind any misunderstandings and miscommunications and sever all soul ties that come to divide us.

Hear my cry, Lord. I pray Your will over his/her life. Break the yoke of fear from his/her neck. Rip the scales of leviathan according to Job 41:15. Rebuke proud and arrogant demons from him/her, in Jesus's name. I loose humbleness and love on him/her. For Your glory, I pray that he/she will walk in the integrity of Your Spirit, be saved, and be set free from his/her enslaved heart. I rebuke his/her ego and the spirits of low self-image, self-rejection, double mindedness, vanity, idolatry, and rebellion, in Jesus's name.

I take authority over these strongmen, in Jesus's name. I bind every spirit of insecurity and inferiority that comes to convince him/her that he's/she's not worth being loved. I break the back of the spirits of self-delusion, self-deception, self-seduction, and lust. I loose the fullness of the Holy Spirit on him/her. I pray that he/she will walk completely in the Spirit of truth and that his/her head will be crowned with the wisdom and understanding of the true and living God.

I speak peace to his/her heart, soul, spirit, and mind. Lord, by Your strength, root out every evil thing from him/her. I pray that he/she will not be shipwrecked but that he/she will walk with a good conscience and remember the true prophecies of God, which were spoken before him/her. I loose obedience on him/her by Your Holy Spirit, in Jesus's name. I decree and declare that the glory of the Lord will be revealed to him/her and that he/she will fall deeply in love with You, Father.

Amen.

PRAYING FOR GOMER'S STRENGTH

Hosea realized that his wife lacked the strength to leave her lifestyle. He always went to her, saved her, and provided a place of rest so that she might be strengthened. She didn't know how or where to seek rest. Torment and humiliation had become her potion. She was weary from her circumstances, disappointments, and abuse. She had yet to experience her own fresh strength from the Lord.

Isaiah 40:29 (KJV) says, "He giveth power to the faint; and to them that have no might he increaseth strength." Hosea understood that when strength is restored, hope is also restored. Hope was what Gomer needed. This hope is birthed by faith through the power of God's love. Hosea's prayer petitioned hope, fresh strength, protection, and an ultimate experience with God. Hosea provided an oasis for Gomer so that she could receive spiritual and natural nourishment.

While Hosea's prayers and declarations of hope over his wife were spurred on by obedience, there is no doubt that he was also moved by pity and compassion to intercede for his lost bride. He entreated God to have mercy on her for every act of ignorance. The story of Hosea and Gomer reveals the power of effective intercession, the plea for exoneration, and the pardoning of sin. It clearly displays Hosea's faithfulness in his effort to buy back his bride in the same way that Christ went to the cross to buy back humankind. It was an unselfish offering of intercession, intervention, and mediation before Abba Father.

Here is the prophecy in Isaiah 53:12 (KJV):

"Therefore, I will divide Him a portion with the great, and he shall divide the spoil with the strong; because He hath poured out his soul unto death; and He was numbered with the transgressors; and He bare the sin of many, made intercession for transgressors."

Chapter 3

THE REFORMING OF GOMER: BEARING THE FRUIT OF REPENTANCE

After I strayed, I repented; after I came to understand, I beat my breast. I was ashamed and humiliated because I bore the disgrace of my youth.

—Jeremiah 31:19 (NIV)

The key to Gomer's deliverance is the same key we can use for our own deliverance—repentance. Hosea 6:1 (NKJV) says, "Come, and let us return to the Lord; for He has torn, but He will heal us." Gomer must be healed, redeemed, restored, and bought back. Even though Gomer repeated her sin, Hosea faithfully brought her back home and to a place that was under his covering so she could repent and start fresh with his love. To retain deliverance (not salvation), Gomer must repent and seek to be married to or in covenant with God.

The apostle Paul explained to the church at Corinth, which was infected by sexual immorality, that its people must live righteously. First Corinthians 6:11 (KJV), "And such were some of you: but ye are washed, but ye are sanctified, but ye are justified in the name of the Lord Jesus, and by the Spirit of our God."

John the Baptist was more than clear about the significance of true repentance. According to Matthew 3, he preached in the wilderness of Judah, saying, "Repent, for the kingdom of heaven is at hand!" He warned the Pharisees and the Sadducees, who were coming to his baptism, to bear fruits worthy of repentance and not to think to say to themselves, *We have Abraham as our father.* Then Jesus said,

> For I say to you that God is able to raise up children of Abraham from these stones. And even now the ax is laid to root of the trees. Therefore, every tree which does not bear good fruit is cut and thrown into the

fire. I indeed baptize your with water unto repentance, but He who is coming after me is mightier than I whose sandals I am not worthy to carry" (Matthew 3:9–11 NKJV)

In this passage of scripture, John the Baptist compares his ministry to God using an ax to clear the orchard of dead wood, especially trees that did not bear the fruit of repentance. He referred to the Pharisees and the Sadducees who came to be baptized as a "brood of vipers!" (verse 7) This elitist group was guilty of pretentious worship in the temple, which led to legalism and the spirit of traditionalism. Even they had to face the eternal judgement of God and His love when they were warned.

John 3:16 (KJV) says, "For God so loved the world that he gave his only begotten Son, that whosoever believeth in him should not perish, but have everlasting life." Most Christians learn this scripture as a child but rarely understand it until they reach maturity. This happens after you meet many failures in life and try to depend upon the world's love, which has waxed cold. Unfortunately, even believers can lose sight of the importance and power of true repentance.

The reformed Gomer understands the need for repentance and the power of atonement. Romans 5:8–10 says,

> But God demonstrates His own love toward us, in that while we were still sinners, Christ died for us. Much more then, having now been justified by His blood, we shall be saved from wrath through Him. For if when we were enemies we were reconciled to God through the death of His Son, much more, having been reconciled, we shall be saved by His life. (NKJV)

This is a glorious revelation to any believer, but in Gomer's case because of her past, it seems to be more than a miracle.

The process of Gomer's reforming bears great fruit through repentance. There is, of course, another process of fruit bearing, the "fruit of the Holy Spirit," which the apostle Paul refers to in his letter to the Galatians. Chapter 5:22–23 says, "But the fruit of the Spirit is love, joy, peace, forbearance, goodness, faithfulness, gentleness and self-control" (NIV). Because of my revelation of Gomer's anointing, I am certain that after the fruit of the Spirit is ripe, other fruit will manifest. This happens because of the ordained call upon a reformed Gomer and the spiritual trauma that he or she has been delivered from.

A TRANSFORMED GOMER

The attributes of a reformed Gomer include passion and worship. After the reforming of Gomer and his or her realization that God has wooed him or her back by His love, the response is deep, passionate, indescribable worship. John 4:24 says, "God is a Spirit: and they that worship him must worship in spirit and truth" (KJV). Gomer now expresses worship that is birthed out of a personal love story with God, who has saved him or her from the pit of whoredom, rejection, and shame.

Gomer remembers the emptiness she was left with after being used for coins. She knows how it felt to pour her soul into a dumb idol and how it now feels to be fully in love with the lover of her soul. She understands the destruction that comes with profane worship. No longer is Gomer's heart enslaved, but now her heart and soul can rejoice as it says in Psalm 103:1, "Bless the Lord, O my soul; And all that is within me, bless His holy name!" (NKJV)

The reformed Gomer's love affair with God causes her to be overwhelmed with goodness and grace. She has come to the full the relevance of unmerited favor from the God of the universe. She is a former wretch who stands under a free-flowing fountain of blessings that has brought her everlasting joy and gladness. She is fully enthralled with the kingdom of God and its benefits. Romans 14:17 says, "For the kingdom of God is not eating and drinking, but righteousness and peace and joy in the Holy Spirit" (NKJV). Now Gomer has put away her selfish desires for the wonder and fulfillment of God's will and plans for her life.

Gomer's transformed life has changed her whole perspective. She seeks God for her purpose and placement. She does things in God's time and His season. Psalm 16:8 says, "I keep my eyes always on the Lord. With him at my right hand, I will not be shaken" (NIV). She is fervent in her obedience because she doesn't want to cause harm to her eternal lover's heart. The fear of not being obedient grips her heart. Her eyes will fill with tears at the thought of rejecting her Lord because she remembers the painful repercussions of disobedience from her past life. Her biggest fear is rebellion, but then she is brought back to a place of peace with the gentle reminder that she is being kept by God.

To be in love with the Father is to be in love with the Son and the Holy Spirit. Great benefits of this everlasting relationship will come. First Peter 1:8–9 says, "Though you have not seen him you love him; and even though you do not see him now, you believe in him and are filled with an inexpressible and glorious joy, for you are receiving the end result of your faith, the salvation of your souls" (NIV). The outcome of our trusting God during the trials of life is our salvation. That is the driving solace in Gomer's deliverance. She is balanced by that.

She is also burdened by the search for and deliverance of bound souls, who have experienced the same shame and pain as she has. While she is walking in the blessings of the Lord, she is humbled by the opportunity to share her story.

Passionate Worship	Overwhelming Grace	Fervent Obedience
Great Humility	Burdened for Souls	Gifted to Reach the Unreachable

PRAYER OF A TRANSFORMED GOMER

Dear Father God,

Forgive me. Who am I but clay? Help me, Lord. Forgive me, Lord, for I am sorry. I repent. I am angry with myself because of my sinful heart. I wanted to sin. I was tormented by my sin. Then I became frustrated by the glimpses of Your promises for me. How can You love me so much? But You do.

I come against the spirit of heaviness that tries to ride me by going through my emotions and is sometimes fed by my own regret. I call my emotions under the submission of the Holy Spirit. Hedge in my mind by the power of the blood of Jesus. Don't let me operate in the wrong spirit. Let my walk be excellent. Cleanse my life from secret faults and selfishness that has risen in me because of my will. I humble myself to Your plans for me. I trust in You.

Amen.

Chapter 4

TODAY'S GOMER: THE REDEEMING OF A GENERATION

When all that generation had been gathered
to their fathers, another generation arose
after them who did not know the Lord
nor the work which He had done for Israel.
(Judges 2:10 NKJV)

Who is Gomer in our current age? She is this generation
of sons and daughters who do not know the God of their
fathers. This can be found in Judges 2:10 (NKJV), where
it says, "When all that generation had been gathered to
their fathers, another generation arose after them who
did not know the Lord nor the work which He had done
for Israel."

Showing its disdain for holiness, this generation has been lulled to sleep by its flesh. This generation of millennials seems intent in their hearts not to connect with God. They are more engaged in connecting with one another virtually and exchanging intellectual thoughts or powerless hashtags about the next big cause. The young people of this generation sweetly surrender their bodies to open expressions of their thoughts through tattoo after tattoo after tattoo.

Today's Gomer is trapped in an identity crisis and is engaged in a war to water down God's Word to fit her unfitness. She has played the harlot to a nation that battles political wars on social media. She is uncovered by the vulgarity and lewdness on the Internet. She is full of fleshly desires and behaves shamefully due to her intoxication with her own enslaved heart and from the offerings of sexual perversion on television and in movies. Today's Gomer doesn't burn incense but offers up the smoke of marijuana, ice, spice, and meth to her idol, Baal.

Is she redeemable? Hosea 11:1–4 (NKJV) declares, "When Israel was a child, I loved him, And out of Egypt I called My son. As they went from them; They sacrificed to the Baals, and burned incense to carved images. I taught Ephraim to walk, taking them by the arms; But they did not know that I healed them. I drew them with gentle cords. With bands of love." Today's Gomer is redeemable because God's love is just as sure as His judgements. Just like Hosea, God has already bought back this current generation through the blood of Jesus Christ.

First Corinthians 7:23 (NKJV) says, "You were bought at a price, do not become slaves of men." God is raising up this generation of sons and daughters to help bring their generation back to God through the Gomer anointing.

Many people in the body of Christ will go forth in this anointing. They understand what it means to worship and offer sensual sacrifices before a dumb idol and then to have the only true and wise God redeem them by the atoning blood of Jesus Christ. They understand what it means to live shamefully before people and to now be free to share their testimonies of a past life of lasciviousness and victory and deliverance in God. They are being set free from their sins and evil ways and are now being catapulted into ministry to help enlarge the kingdom of God.

Today's Gomer is just like the biblical Gomer. At

first, she doesn't see the need to be rescued and then doesn't think she can be rescued. Who can understand the emptiness that she feels? She uses the bounty of her harlotry to try to fill the void in her soul. She is bewitched by her search to fill a longing of which she cannot find the words to explain.

Psalm 106:6 (NKJV) says, "We have sinned with our fathers, We have committed iniquity, We have done wickedly. Our fathers in Egypt did not understand Your wonders; They did not remember the multitude of Your mercies." Here lies the answer as to who is at fault for the harlotry of today's Gomer. This generation has lived up to what the Word of God says about being weaker and wiser. However, the harlotry we see today didn't start with this generation but with past generations. God's common grace still keeps the world turning as He waits for His people to know Him and to follow hard after Him. He saves them by His redeeming love. Psalm 106:8 (NKJV) says, "Nevertheless He saved them for His name's sake that He might make His mighty power known."

THE ANOINTING OF GOMER

When I pursued this revelation God had given me regarding the anointing of Gomer, I met other people's strongholds. The hows and whys enlightened me but also saddened me. I found the limiting of God's power by the church and the sin of man to be great, as if the redeeming blood of the Lamb of God, Jesus, who had been slain, had never been shed. It reminded me of when the apostle Paul warned his spiritual son, Timothy, about believers who would put on a form of religiousness but deny the power of God (see 2 Timothy 3:5).

An empty religion is like serving an idol or forgetting we are in a relationship with God. What makes a believer think he or she can have it all together in Christ? What makes the next person, who is considered to have somewhat greater sin, think he or she cannot do this?

The anointing of Gomer is awesome when Gomer is delivered from the most unspeakable evils. It is an anointing that today's Gomer carries because she was once naked and lewd but is now clothed in righteousness and wears the spiritual garments of a prince or princess. This anointing will help today's Gomer carry her testimony to the ends of the earth if she thinks it will touch the life of one soul and cause it to find freedom by salvation through Christ Jesus. This anointing makes Gomer immune to the whispers of those who know her and her past. This anointing carries great deliverance to those who encounter the redeemed Gomer and her spiritual gifting. Whether through song, preaching, teaching, or an encouraging word, deliverance has gone forth, in that moment of shared grace, to those who are lost and don't have a clue about their conditions. Gomer discerns their brokenness because she has been there.

PRAYER FOR THIS GENERATION

Lord, my God,

I lift the young people of this generation up to You. You know their hearts and their pain. They are hurting from the bondage of sin and are unaware that they need a Savior. Lord, touch their minds and hearts. Draw them by Your Spirit. Root out the spirit of double mindedness, whoredom, perversion, lust, and addiction. I apply the blood of Jesus to their souls. Wash them only as You can. Forgive them of their transgressions and open their hearts to receive Your forgiveness.

Let them feel Your love. Root out self-deception, inner hurt, abuse, grief, sorrow, shame, guilt, and pride. I release the Holy Spirit, for He is a comforter and a teacher. I loose salvation, healing, the freedom of your Spirit, and strength to their hearts and minds. May they become new creations in Christ Jesus.

Amen.

PRAYER OF REFORMED GOMER

My God,

I ask You to order my steps in Thy Holy Word. Let not my past iniquity have dominion over me. Great are your tender mercies. Please quicken me according to your judgments. My eyes are focused unto the hills from where my help comes from. Lord, may I keep your peace. May I learn Your ways. Thank You for favoring me. I now have respect for Your ways and delight in them. I will not forget Your Word and

Your love, which is pure. I open myself to Your righteousness. Yes, I receive. My heart is fixed.

I will only look to You. I give You the praise for You are the lover of my soul and my will is to please You. I submit to You and not to a lover from my past. I will keep Your words. Thank You for having precious thoughts toward me. Help me not to lean on my own understanding, but let me be happy in Your wisdom and understanding. Let Your wisdom crown my head as an ornament of grace, for Your glory. Use me and add Your strength for me to go and do what You have called me to do in Your kingdom.

Help me to accomplish my kingdom mission for Your glory. I am small in stature, yet by Your strength, I'm Your giant. By Your Spirit, You have chosen me. Help me not to fear, for in You there is no failure or regret. Help me to speak only what You say. You have anointed me with Your power and have given me great deliverance. Thank You for granting me the strength to bring forth my destiny for Your glory and my good. I ask this all in the strong name of Jesus.

Amen.

Chapter 5

A MINISTRY OF HOPE

Now Jabez was more honorable than his brothers, and his mother called his name Jabez, saying, "Because I bore him in pain. And Jabez called on the God of Israel saying, Oh, that You would bless me indeed, and enlarge my territory, that Your hand would be with me, and that You would keep me from evil, that I may not cause pain! So God granted him what he requested."

—1 Chronicles 4:9–10 (NKJV)

The body of Christ must be mindful that it exists in a society that manufactures false hope, thereby producing false expectations, which are fueled by vanity, idolatry, and greed. This creates a generation that is confused and at it core, is hopeless.

Gomer understands what it feels like to drown in hopelessness and be blinded by the counterfeit success that the world has to offer this generation. The apostle Peter gave a clarion call to God's people in 1 Peter 1:13 (NKJV): "Therefore gird up the loins of your mind, be sober, and rest your hope fully upon the grace that is to be brought to you at the revelation of Jesus Christ." This unconnected generation needs the revelation of Jesus that produces hope and holy living, which are essential for all believers.

The apostle Peter's instructions are clear. First, we must get our minds right. Yes, holy living starts in the mind. We must think clearly about the Word of God by meditating on it and connecting it to our hearts. God's Word is truth and our hope will be sustained in truth.

Secondly, we must get control of our flesh by being sober. We cannot be careless and become intoxicated with the cares of life. That will only choke out the Word and our hope in it. It takes us down the road of temptation, foolishness, unfruitfulness, and hurtful lust, which could lead us away from our faith in Christ and from His church.

Thirdly, we must rest or place our hope in the grace of God—His unmerited favor—thereby gaining an appreciation for God's great grace. By accomplishing this, we are open to a desire for God and an expectation of what He is going to do in us. This is for every believer.

So this takes us back to the introduction of this book when I asked the question, "Can Gomer lead worship?" Now I am asking, can Gomer preach? Can she teach? Can she evangelize? By now, I pray you can see that she most definitely can.

Gomer transformed is a true denominator in a generation that has no desire to be connected to the true and living God. Why? She was just like this generation. She was not properly introduced to the relational and loving God but to the idols of this world. Like Gomer, this generation has been marginalized by the church.

The anointing, which God has equipped Gomer with for ministry, will not stand for ostracism and silence. The converted Gomer steers clear of being imprisoned mentally with strongholds regarding her past life. The past is an issue that every believer must face. It can be detrimental and affect the flourishment of ministry.

As believers, we have to accept and understand who we are in Christ. As it is revealed in Colossians 1:27

(KJV), "To whom God would make known what is the riches of the glory of this mystery among the Gentiles; which is Christ in you, the hope of glory." Christ in us allows us to share in the glory of God. The expectation of what God is going to do in us and through us is part of what encourages us in our journey in life and is our hope.

Gomer has hope for this generation and can discern its pains, fears, and frustrations. It's really simple and amazing all at the same time. When we come out of sin, we come into hope. The trauma of our sins can leave mental marks embedded in our minds—the haunting fear that we might go back into our awful past sins. We must be careful not to feed our fears. We shouldn't allow others to feed our fears and condemnation when they won't acknowledge our deliverance. Only our hearts can understand the importance and pureness of the deliverance that has taken place in our lives. No one can take that experience from us. No one can water down the power of God that has moved in our lives. We are in a relationship with Jesus Christ, and nothing can take that away from us.

Unfortunately, some church cultures try to keep Gomer quiet, sitting on the sidelines, and waiting and waiting for a chance to get in the game, so to speak. I may seem critical of the church at this point, but it's really an observation that makes me sad. In ministry, I witness numerous people carrying words from God that affirm their purposes and destinies. I have also seen the body of Christ do its best to kill those words with tradition, legalism, nepotism, self-righteousness, and exclusion, just to keep their clichés safe.

Please understand that if you are in church, you have been found guilty of it, whether by omission or commission. Maybe we do this because we had to go through it to prove ourselves to others. There is no time for this in the body of Christ for the world urgently needs what the church has to offer: hope in Jesus Christ. This hope must be carried to every nation, marketplace, prison, palace, slum, and ghetto of the world.

No one can keep you from your destiny except you. However, your adversary will use whomever and whatever to try to convince you that you are not worthy or equipped for the calling on your life. The enemy would like nothing better than to encourage you to forfeit your future, your authentic self, and God's plans for your life. This is especially true of someone like Gomer, right? Who believes that she can recover and that God can restore her life from harlotry and idolatry? That would take a miracle. Thankfully, God specializes in bringing forth miracles in our lives every day.

When the church marginalizes or downgrades a person who has come from a past of debauchery, it declares subconsciously that our God is not strong enough to deliver people from their pasts. The church is then questioning the sovereignty of God. It is questioning His work and doubting His ability to save.

God asked his servant Job an astonishing question in Job 38:4 (NIV): "Where were you when I laid the foundations of the earth?" I have great appreciation for this portion of scripture because it reveals the ignorance humans have regarding the sovereignty of God. It should lead us to a place of humility.

Who are we that we can question His providential works? It is the same question the body of Christ should ask when it begins to marginalize a person with thoughts that are based on what is known of his or her past. Where were you when Gomer was enslaved in sin? Where were you when she cried out for her voided soul's remedy? Where were you when she chose to believe by faith in the promises and prophecies of God over her life? Where were you?

Romans 8:28 (NKJV) says, "And we know that all things work together for good to those who love God, to those who are the called according to His purpose." God is the author of humankind's purposes. Because of God the Father's glorious plan of salvation through Jesus Christ, we can walk, talk, and live fully by believing in an expected end and directing the world to it. We must trust in and love God, who has called us to fulfill His purpose for His glory, which will be revealed in the earth. Gomer is called and has virtue to succeed in ministry as well.

PRAYER FOR LEADERSHIP IN THE BODY OF CHRIST

Dear God,

I lift up to You this day, every leader in my life, in my church, and in the body of Christ. Lord, humble us by the power of the Holy Spirit. Teach us understanding and wisdom and grant us great rest in Your truth and Your ways. May our strength be renewed, and may we walk in the fullness of obedience to You. May we cast down our selfish ambitions, selfish desires, and self-importance. Help up to discern with love, hope, and faith by Your Spirit. Lord, anoint our conversations and help us to act correctly. May we truly walk by the fruit of the Spirit and full of power and authority.

May we seek authentic forgiveness when we have brought offence to a brother or a sister. Reveal our own hearts to us, that we may be free from our own vices. Help us to lift up the body of Christ in prayer and love. Show Your glory to us. Show Your glory to Your people. Show Yourself to be strong in our lives. Shine in our lives. The heavens declare Your glory, my God. You reign forever! Show Your glory through Your people, oh God. Let Your kingdom birth sons and daughters from us for Your glory and our good.

Amen.

Notes

INTRODUCTION

1 Jewish Virtual Library, "Encyclopedia Judaica: Baal Worship," https:// www.jewishvirtuallibrary.org/baal-worship-jewish-virtual-library.

2 American Tract Society Bible Dictionary, "Baal," StudyLight.Org, https://www.studylight.org/dictionaries/ats/b/baal.html.

CHAPTER 1

1 Jewish Virtual Library, "Encyclopedia Judaica: Baal Worship," https:// www.jewishvirtuallibrary.org/baal-worship-jewish-virtual-library.

2 American Tract Society Bible Dictionary, "Baal," StudyLight.Org, https://www.studylight.org/dictionaries/ats/b/baal.html.

CPSIA information can be obtained
at www.ICGtesting.com
Printed in the USA
BVHW032125011019
559980BV00001B/51/P